SCHOLASTIC

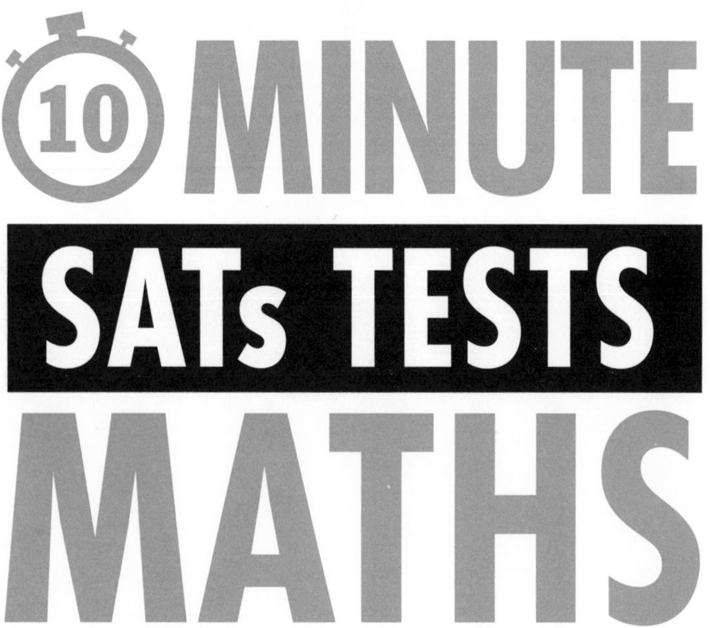

10 Minute SATs Tests Maths

AGES 6–7
YEAR 2

KS1

Scholastic Education, an imprint of Scholastic Ltd
Book End, Range Road, Witney, Oxfordshire, OX29 0YD
Registered office: Westfield Road, Southam, Warwickshire CV47 0RA
www.scholastic.co.uk

2 3 4 5 6 6 7 8 9 0 1 2 3 4 5 6
British Library Cataloguing-in-Publication Data
A catalogue record for this book is available from the British Library.

ISBN 9781407176093

Printed and bound in China by Hung Hing Offset Printing

Author
Tim Handley

Editorial
Audrey Stokes, Mary Nathan, Julia Roberts

Cover and Series Design
Scholastic Design Team: Nicolle Thomas and Neil Salt

Design
Scholastic Design Team: Neil Salt and Alice Duggan

Cover Illustration
Adam Linley @ Beehive Illustration, Visual Generation @ Shutterstock

Illustrations
Adam Linley/Beehive Illustration and Matt Ward/Beehive Illustration

Contents

How to use this book

This book contains nine different sets of maths tests for Year 2, each containing SATs-style questions. Each set comprises an arithmetic test and a reasoning test, worth 16 marks in total. As a whole, the complete set of tests provides full coverage of the test framework for this age group, across the following strands of the maths curriculum: Number; Calculations; Fractions; Measurement; Geometry; Statistics.

Some questions require a selected response, where children choose the correct answer from several options. Other questions require a constructed response, where children work out and write down their own answer.

A mark scheme, skills check and progress chart are also included towards the end of this book.

Completing the tests

- It is intended that children will take around ten minutes to complete each set of two tests; however, timings at this age are not strict, so allow your child as much time as they need.
- After your child has completed each set, mark the tests and together identify and practise any areas where your child is less confident. Ask them to complete the next set at a later date, when you feel they have had enough time to practise and improve.

SET A

Test 1: Arithmetic

Marks

1. $4 + 1 =$ [5]

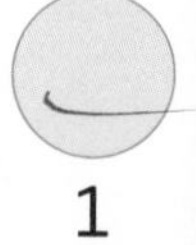

1

2. $22 - 7 =$ [15]

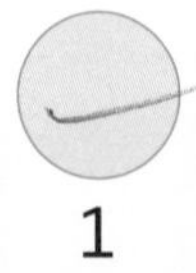

1

3. $12 +$ [4] $= 16$

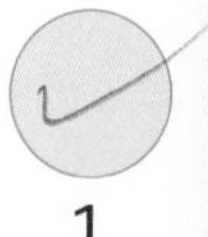

1

Marks

4. $6 \times 10 =$ 60

1

5. 70 $- 30 = 40$

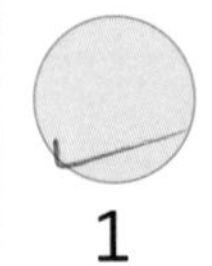
1

6. $76 + 15 =$ 91

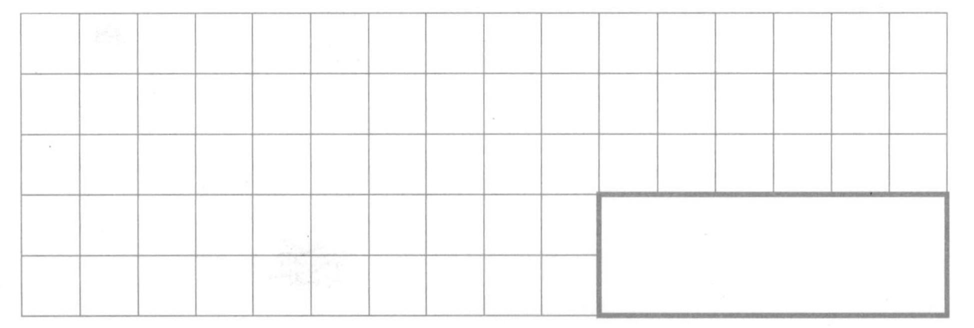

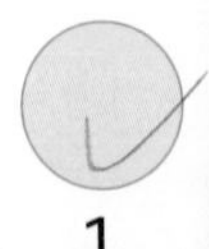
1

SET A

Test 2: Reasoning

Marks

1. Here are some signs.

Write the correct sign in each box.

One has been done for you.

6 [+] 5 = 11

8 [−] 3 = 5 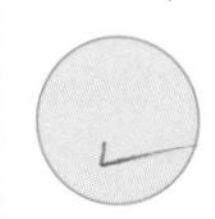 1

9 [+] 3 = 12 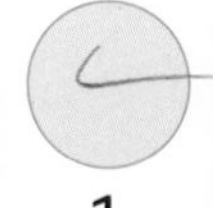 1

---

2. How heavy is this box?

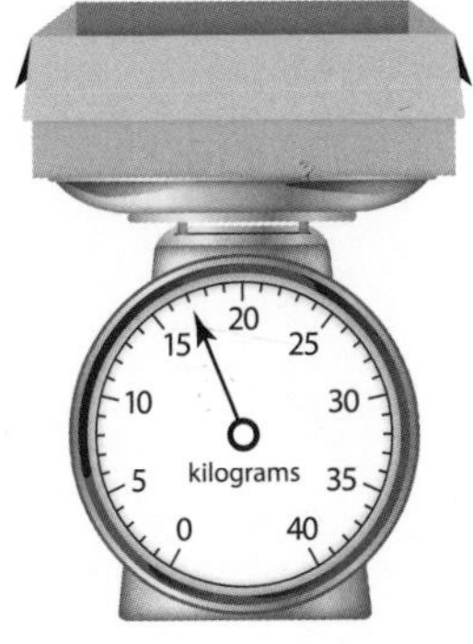

  1

Kian's box is 4 kilograms heavier.

How heavy is Kian's box?

 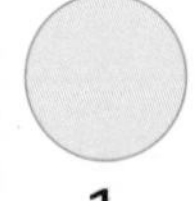 1

Marks

3. Tick the shapes that are **pentagons**.

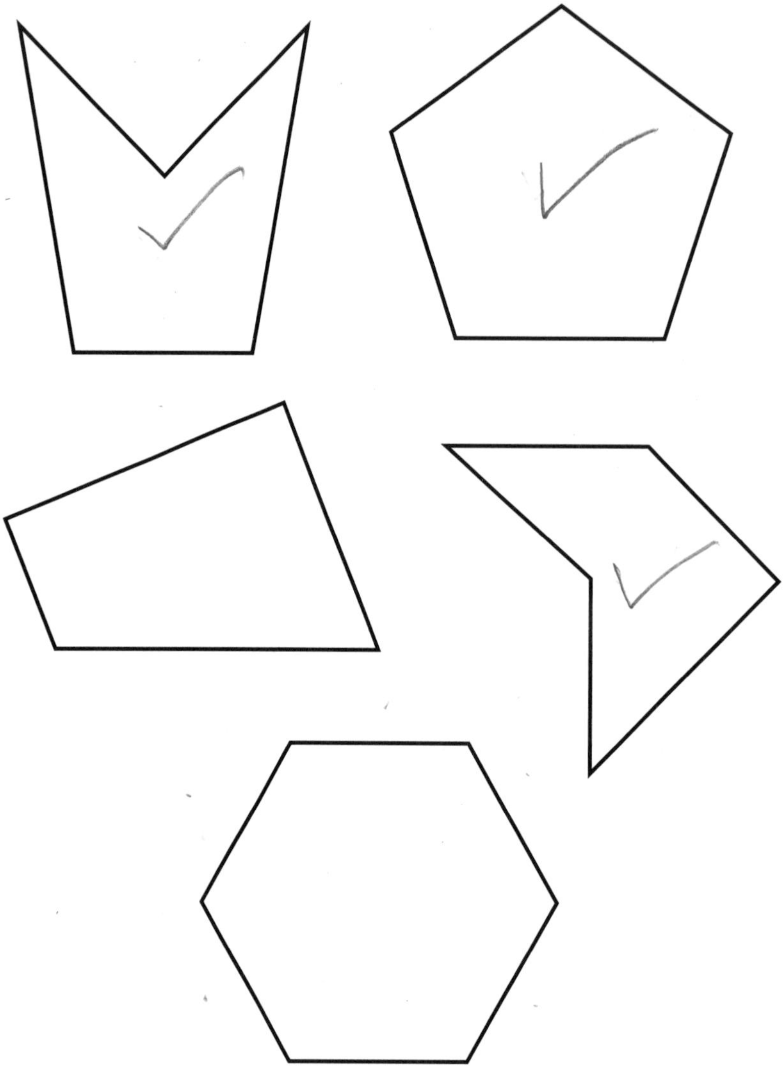

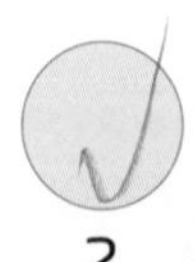

2

Marks

4. Draw a line to join each fraction to its place on the number line.

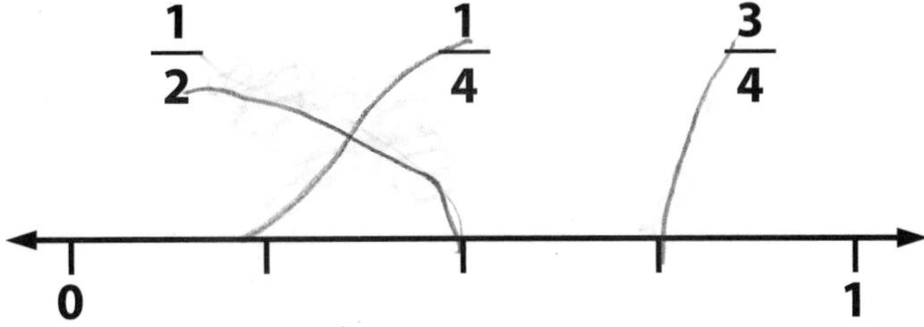

2

5. In Ling's class there are 13 boys and 17 girls.

How many children are in Ling's class?

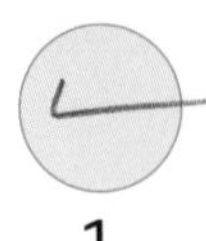

1

How many **more** girls are there than boys?

1

Well done! END OF SET A!

SET B

Test 1: Arithmetic

Marks

1. 9 + 2 = 11

1

2. 50 ÷ 10 = 1

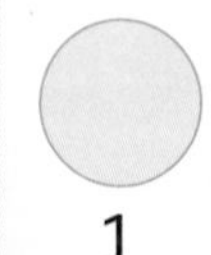
1

3. 4 + 5 + 6 = 15

1

4. $6 \times 2 =$ 12

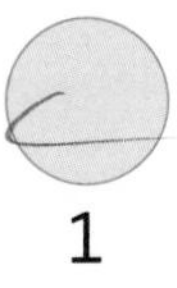

1

5. $\frac{1}{2}$ of 18 = 9

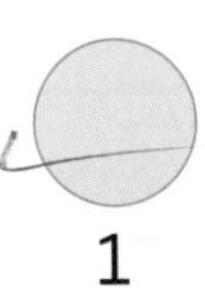

1

6. $77 - 18 =$ 59

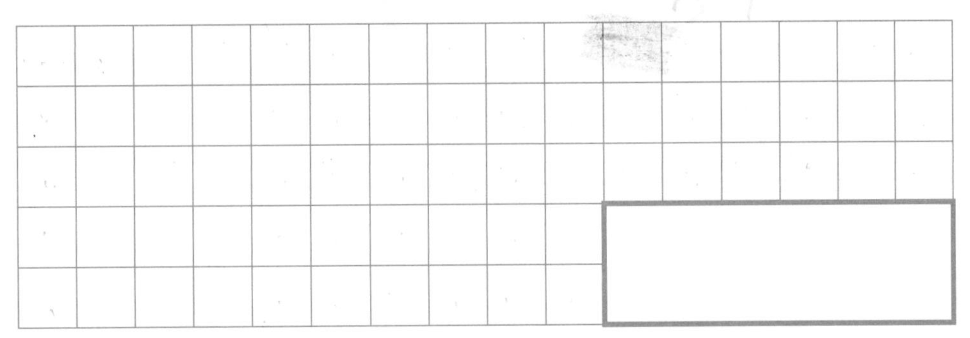

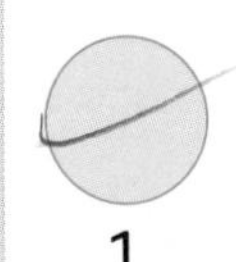

1

SET B

Test 2: Reasoning

Marks

1. Look at these shapes.

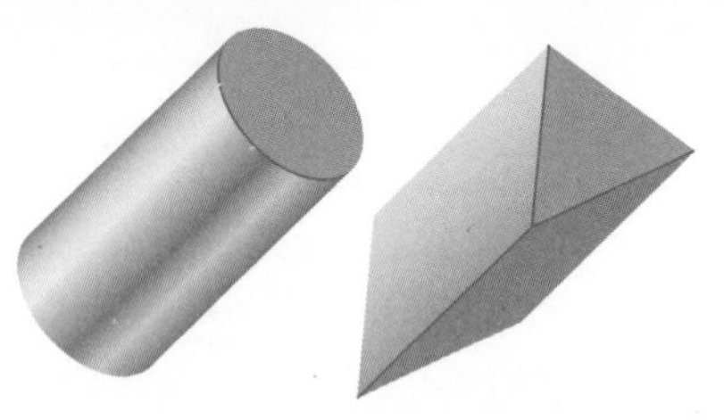

How many vertices, faces and edges does each shape have?

Write the numbers into the table. Some numbers have been filled in for you.

Shape	Number of vertices	Number of faces	Number of edges
Cylinder	0	3	2
Triangular prism	6	5	9

2

2. Complete the number sequence.

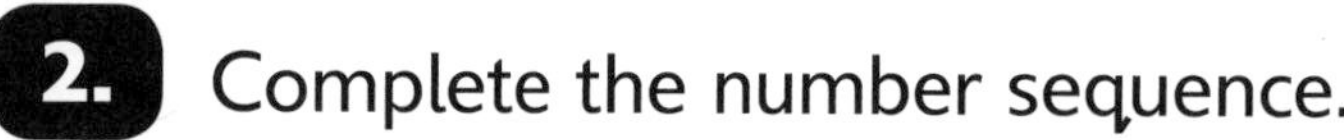

3, 6, [9], 12, 15, [18], 21

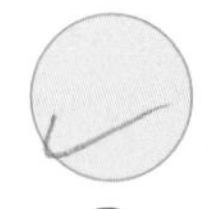

2

3. Write these numbers in order from **smallest** to **largest**.

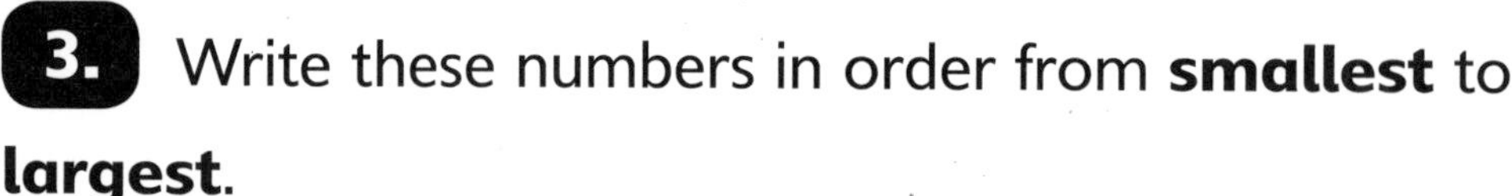

12 54 45 56 32 23

The first two have been done for you.

[12] [23]  [32]  [45]  [54]  [56]

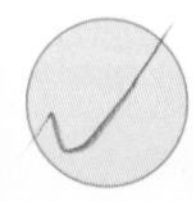

1

Marks

4. In Miss Sparrow's class, each table seats 6 children.

There are enough chairs for every child.

There are 5 tables.

How many children are in Miss Sparrow's class?

1

5. This shape has been divided into equal parts.

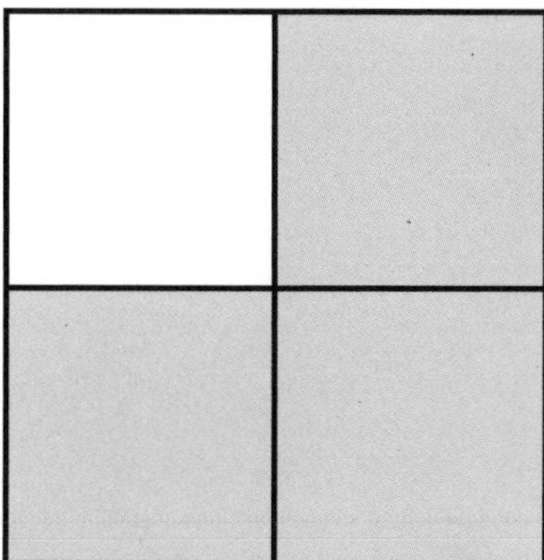

What fraction of the shape is shaded?

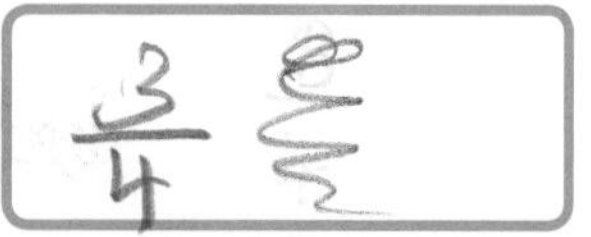

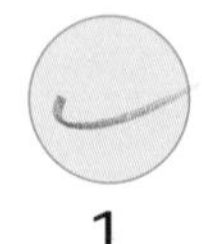

1

Marks

6. Sophie has these coins.

How much money does Sophie have?

1

7. Look at this **addition**.

$$8 + 7 = 15$$

Use the numbers from the addition above to make these calculations correct.

☐ + 8 = ☐

1

☐ − 7 = ☐

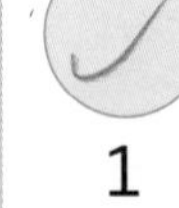

1

Well done! END OF SET B!

SET C

Test 1 : Arithmetic

Marks

1. $8 - 2 = \square$

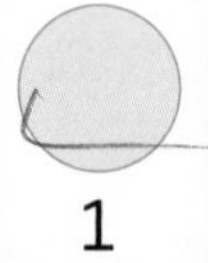

1

2. $45 \div 5 = \square$

1

3. $6 \times \square = 60$

1

Marks

4. $\frac{3}{4}$ of 12 = ☐

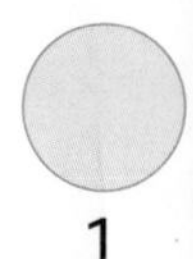

1

5. 69 + 17 = ☐

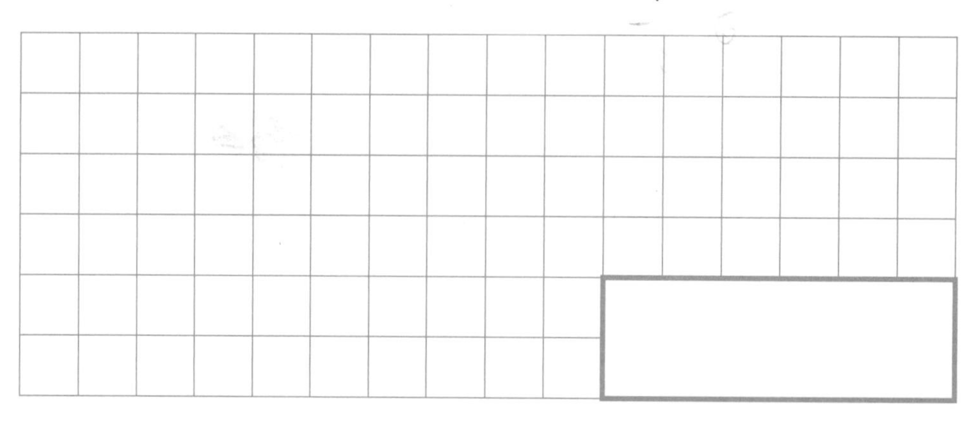

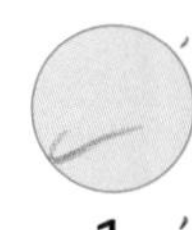

1

6. 10 ÷ 2 = ☐

1

SET C

Test 2: Reasoning

Marks

1. Amir has used place value blocks to show two numbers.

What are the numbers?

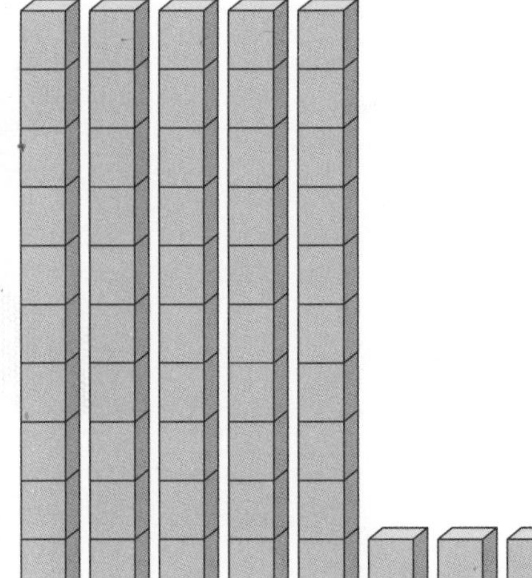

57

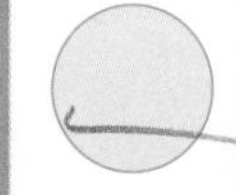

1

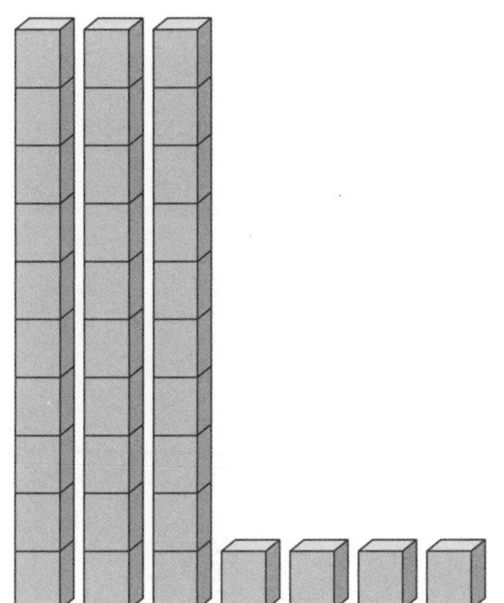

34

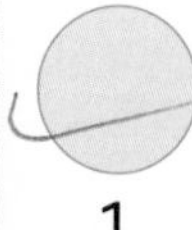

1

Marks

2. Charlotte is counting in multiples of 3.

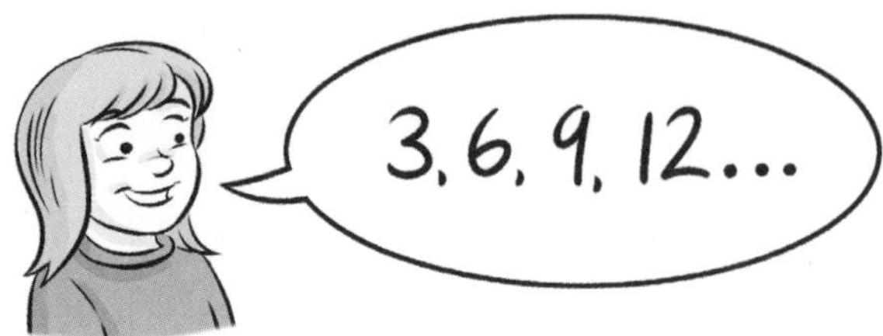

What is the next number that she will say?

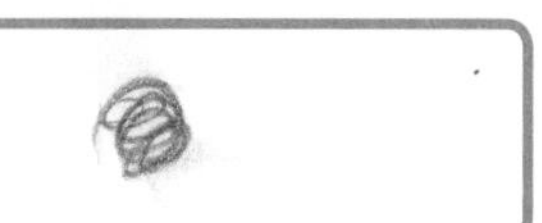

1

Amir is counting backwards from 20 in multiples of 2

What is the next number that he will say?

1

---

3. Write **in words** the number that is **10 more** than 13

1

Write **in words** the number that is **10 less** than 24

1

Marks

4. Kian, Ling and Charlotte grew sunflowers.

They record how tall their sunflowers are in a table.

Name	Height of sunflower
Kian	32cm
Ling	29cm
Charlotte	23cm

Whose sunflower is the tallest?

1

How much taller is Ling's sunflower than Charlotte's sunflower?

cm

1

5. Josh has 24 football cards.

He gives $\frac{1}{4}$ of them to Kian.

How many cards does Josh give to Kian?

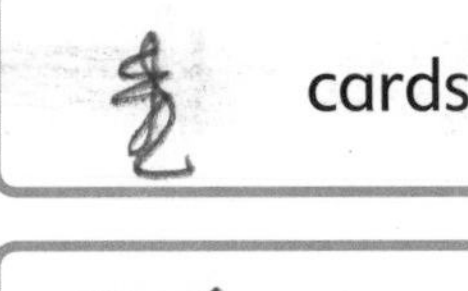
cards

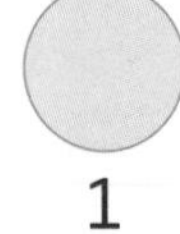
1

How many cards does Josh have left?

cards

1

Well done! END OF SET C!

SET D

Test 1: Arithmetic

Marks

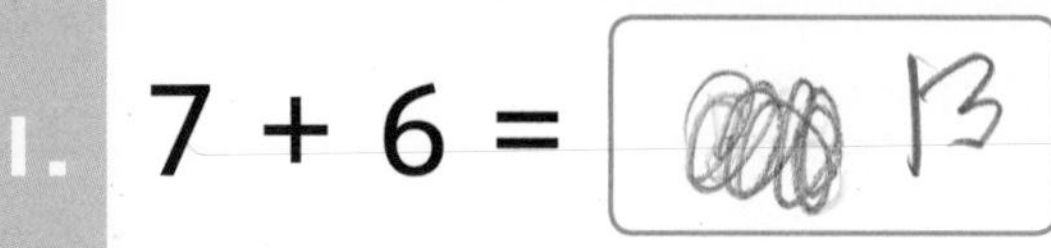

1. $7 + 6 = \square$

1

2. $8 + \square = 19$

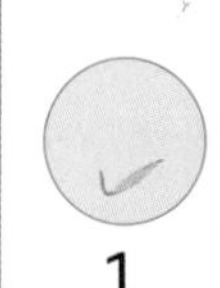

1

3. $8 \times 5 = \square$

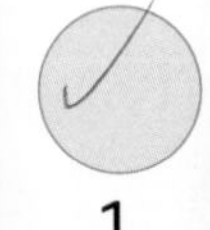

1

Marks

4. $\frac{1}{3}$ of 21 = 7

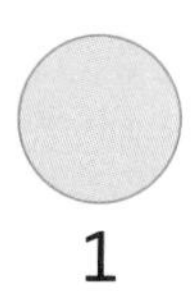
1

5. 87 − 28 = 59

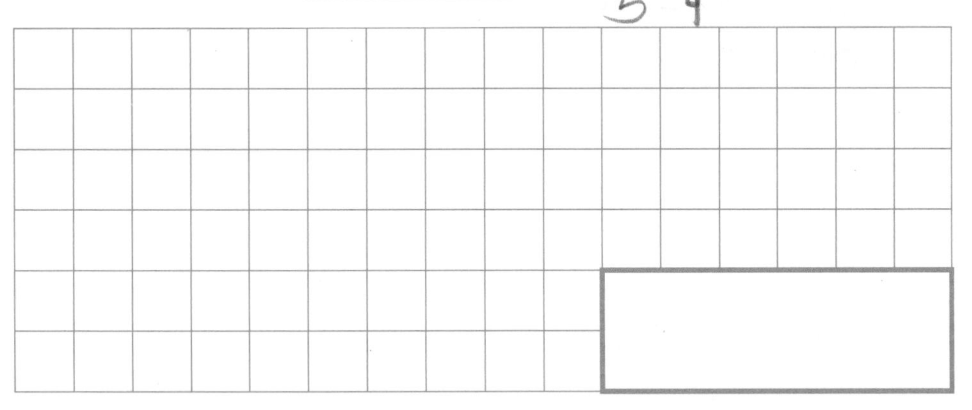

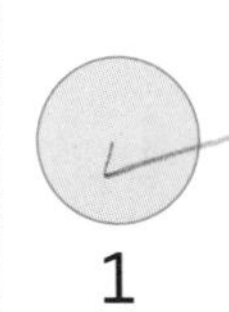
1

6. 16 ÷ 2 =

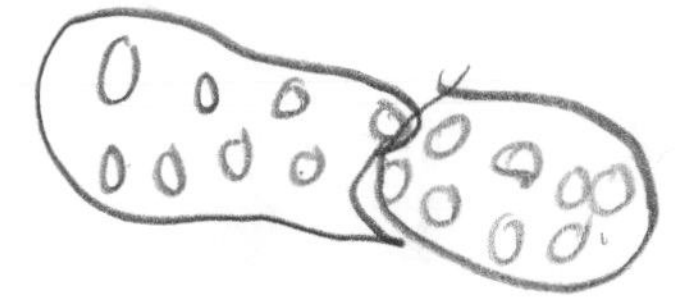

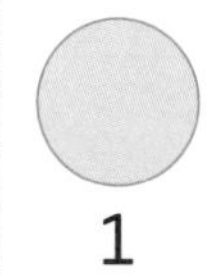
1

SET D

Test 2: Reasoning

Marks

1. Complete the table.

The first row has been done for you.

10 less	Number	10 more
24	34	44
98	109	119
97	107	117

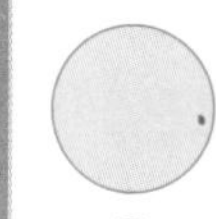
2

2. Sophie knows this multiplication fact.

$$12 \times 2 = 24$$

Use this to complete these calculations.

$2 \times 12 =$ 24

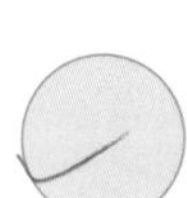

1

$24 \div 2 =$ 12

1

10 MINS

Marks

3. Amir draws a pattern by turning a shape a quarter turn clockwise each time.

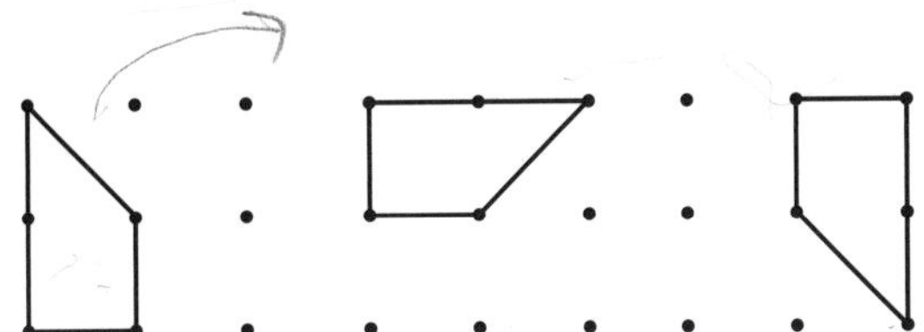

What is the fourth shape in his pattern? Tick the correct shape.

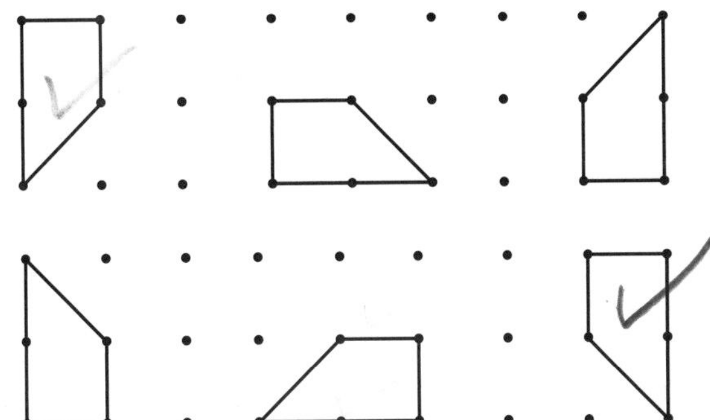

1

What is the fifth shape in his pattern? Tick the correct shape.

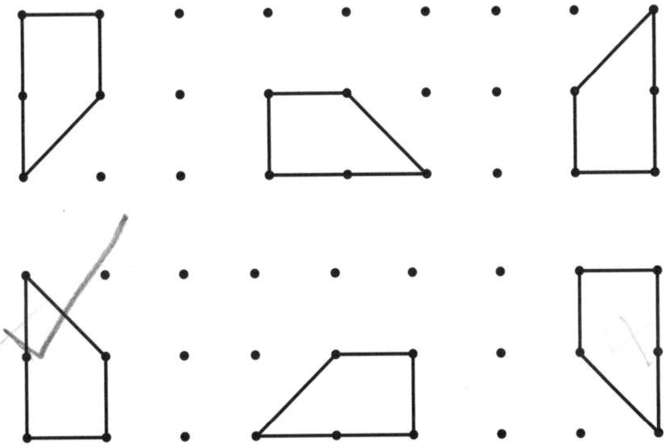

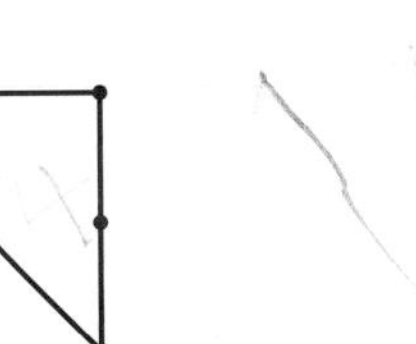

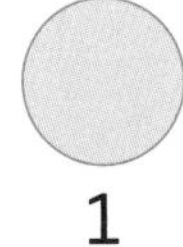

1

Marks

4. Draw hands on the clock to show the time that playtime will start.

2

5. There are 28 children in Josh's class.

He can invite $\frac{3}{4}$ of them to his birthday party.

How many children can he invite?

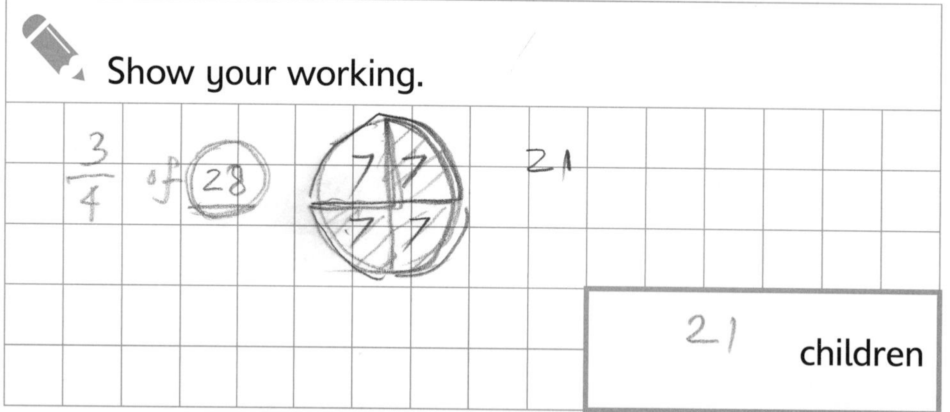

2

Well done! END OF SET D!

SET E

Test 1: Arithmetic

Marks

1. 9 − 4 = [5]

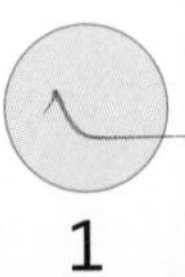

1

2. [25] − 12 = 13 +12

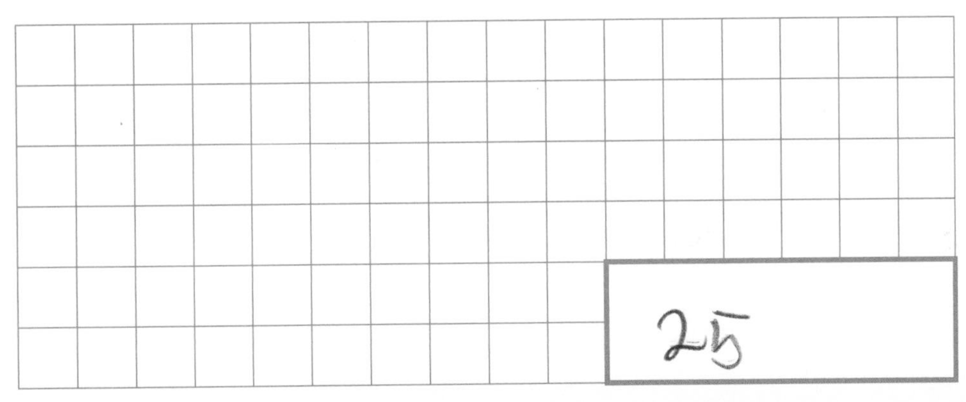

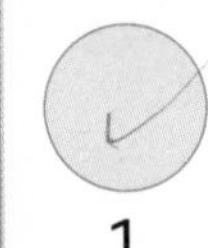

1

3. 10 × 10 = [100]

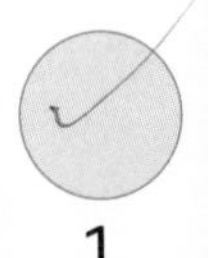

1

Marks

4. $\frac{1}{4}$ of 40 = 

1

5. 90 − 30 =

1

6. 15 ÷ 3 =

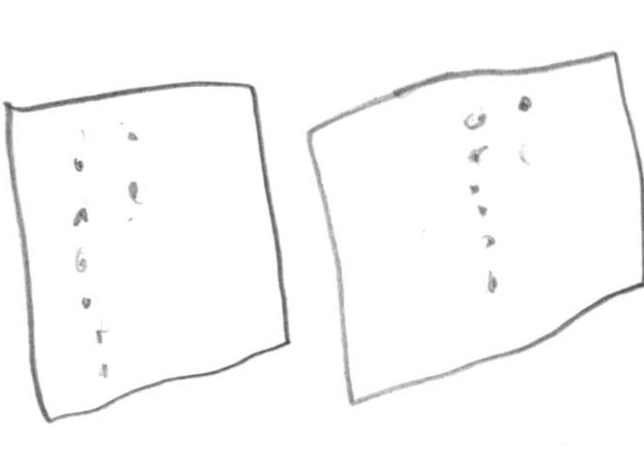

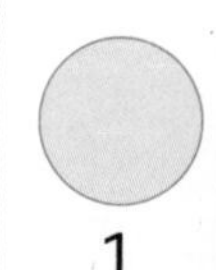

1

SET E

Test 2: Reasoning

Marks

1. Sophie has 17 pens.

Here are Amir's pens.

How many pens does Amir have?

 pens

1

2. Josh is sorting pencils into pots.

Each pot holds 4 pencils.

Josh fills 5 pots.

How many pencils does he use to fill the pots?

 pencils

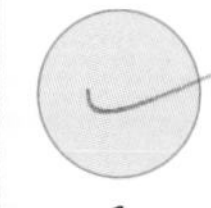

1

3. Use a ruler to measure the length of Ling's toy cat.

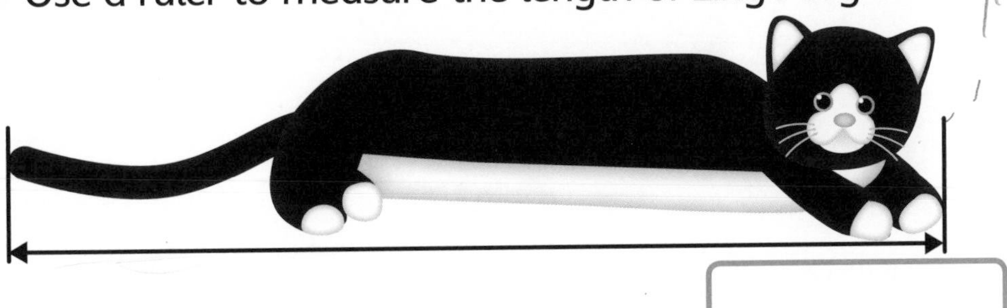

cm

1

10 MINS

Marks

4. Sophie and Kian are playing 'Guess my shape'.

Sophie says, 'My shape has 5 straight sides, but they are not all the same length.'

Tick Sophie's shape below.

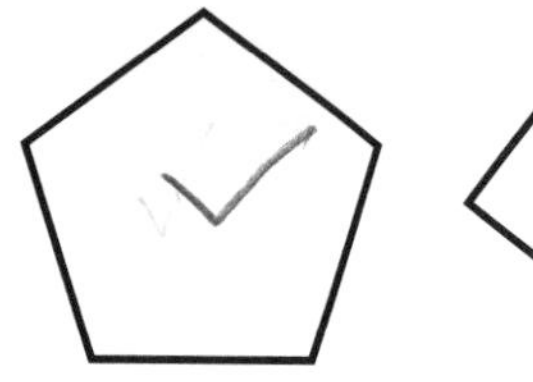

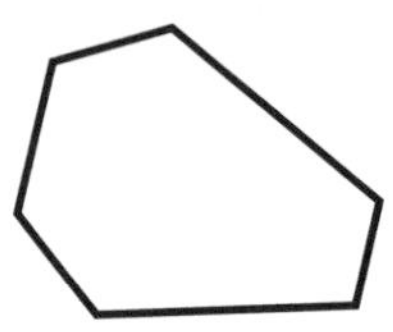

1

Kian says, 'My shape has 4 straight sides, which are all the same length.'

Tick Kian's shape below.

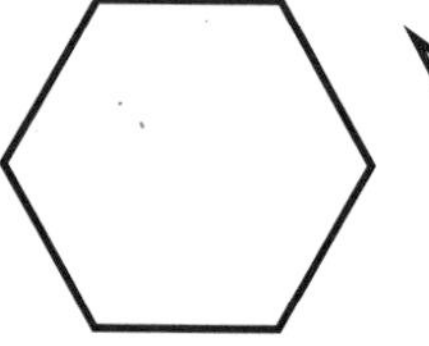
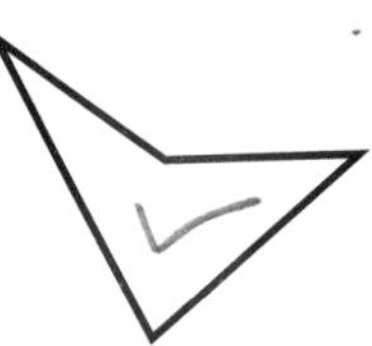

1

---

5. Josh has a piece of paper.

Josh cuts it into quarters.

How many small pieces of paper does he then have?

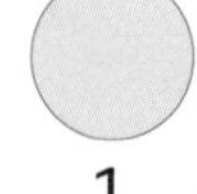
1

Marks

6. This is Ling's purse.

She spends 35p on sweets.

How much money does she have left in her purse?

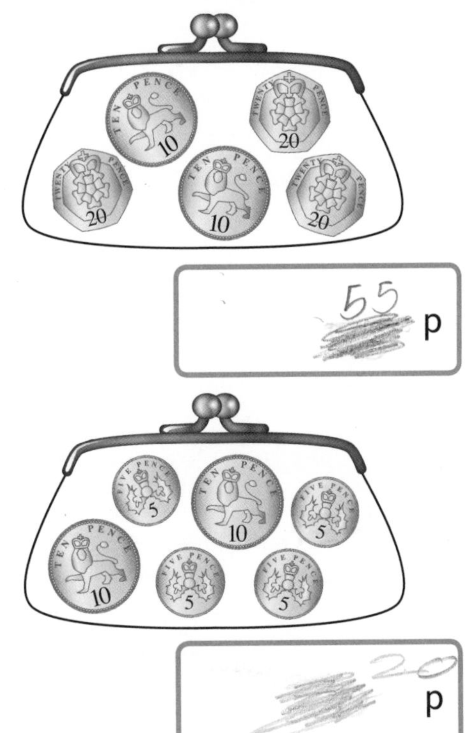

55 p

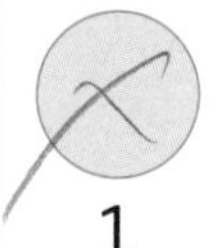

1

This is Charlotte's purse.

She spends **half** her money on sweets.

How much money does she spend on sweets?

20 p

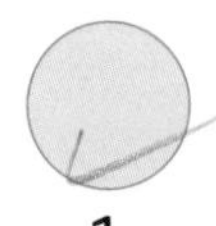

1

7. Josh has 50 sweets to give out at his birthday party.

He gives out 2 sweets to each of his 12 friends.

How many sweets does he have left?

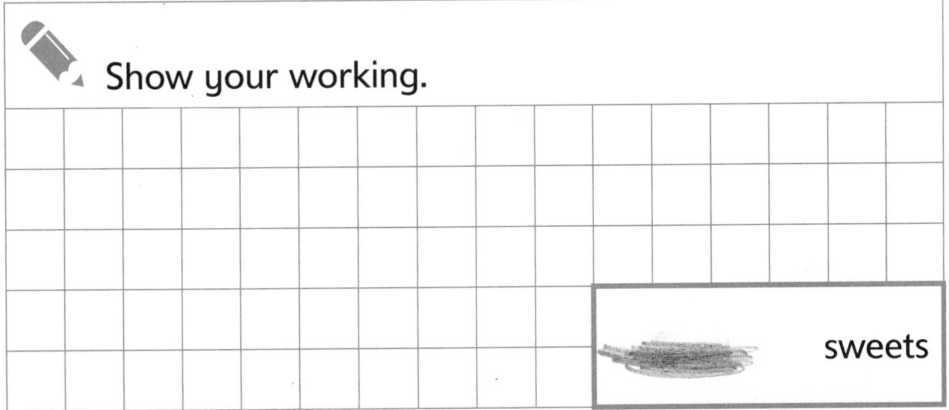

2

Well done! END OF SET E!

SET F

Test 1: Arithmetic

Marks

1. $15 - 5 =$ [10]

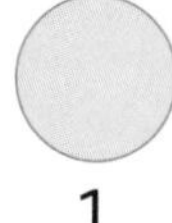

1

2. [6] $+ 8 = 14$

1

3. $41 + 20 =$ [61]

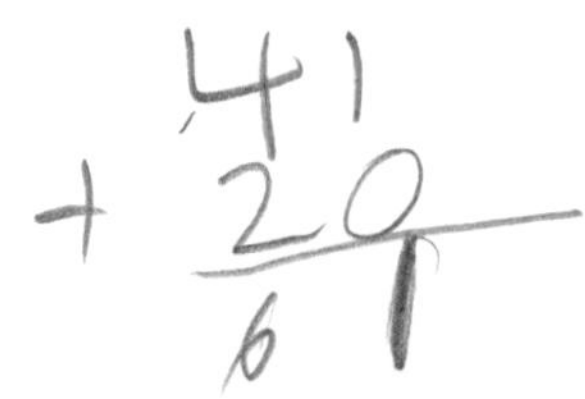

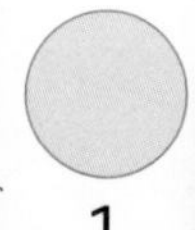

1

Marks

4. $\frac{1}{4}$ of 4 = ☐

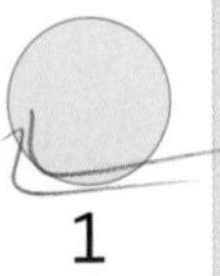
1

5. 56 + 36 = ☐

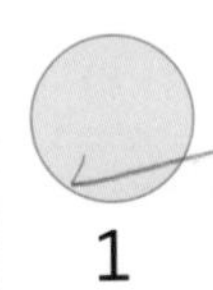
1

6. 20 ÷ 5 = ☐

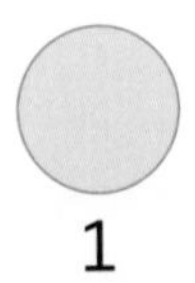
1

Test F

Test 2: Reasoning

Marks

1. Complete the sequence.

14 [ ] 18 [ ] 22

1

2. Kian has worked out this addition.

43 + 22 = 65

Write two subtractions he could use to check his answer.

[ ] – [ ] = [ ]

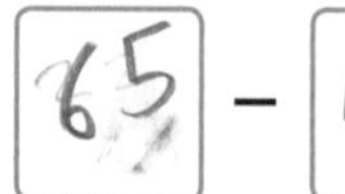

[ ] – [ ] = [ ]

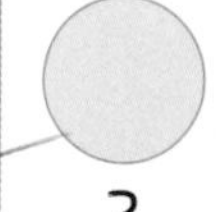

2

Marks

3. This pictogram shows how Mrs Raven's class come to school.

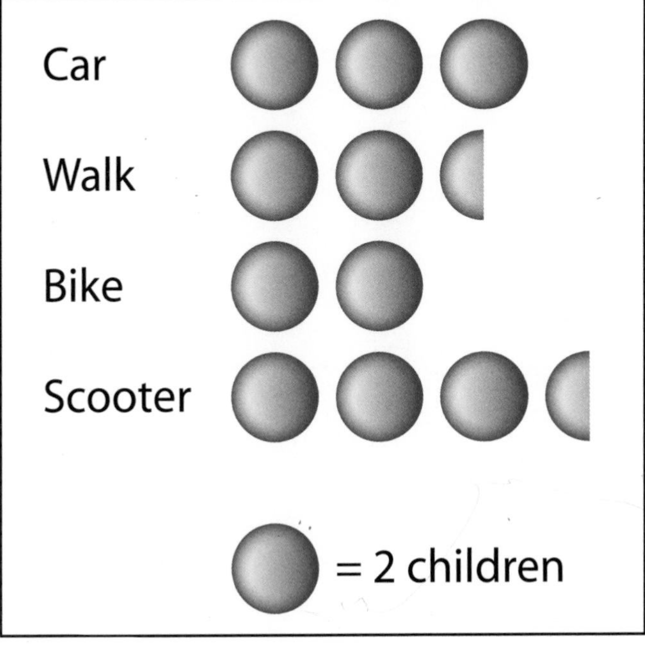

How many children walk to school?

1

How many more children come to school by scooter than come to school by bike?

children

1

SET F

Test 2: Reasoning

Marks

4. Sophie has made a pattern.

Draw in the missing shapes.

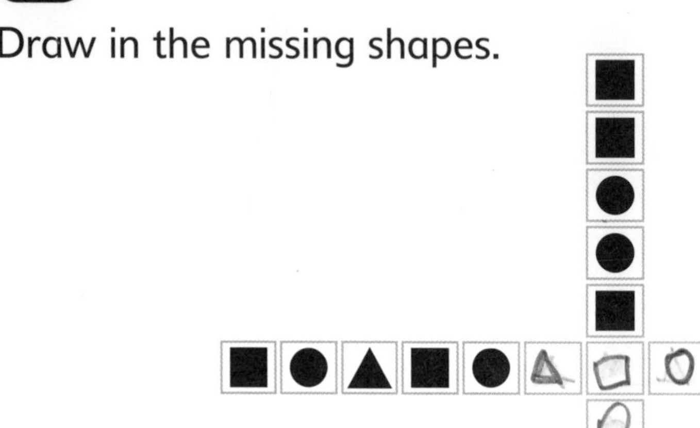

2

5. These are the masses of different baby dinosaurs.

Complete the sentences below to compare the mass of the baby dinosaurs. Use these signs: **< > =**

t-rex ☐ triceratops

1

t-rex ☐ diplodocus

1

How much heavier is a diplodocus than a triceratops?

1

Well done! END OF SET F!

SET G

Test 1: Arithmetic

10 MINS

Marks

1. 8 + 6 = [14]

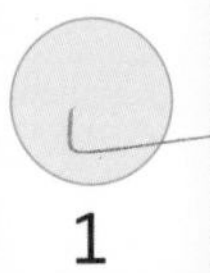

1

2. 8 = 4 + [4]

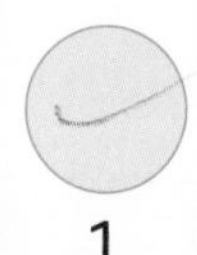

1

3. 62 − 30 = [32]

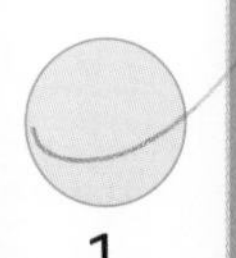

1

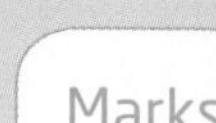

4. $\frac{3}{4}$ of 24 = ☐

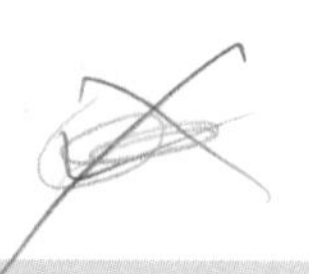

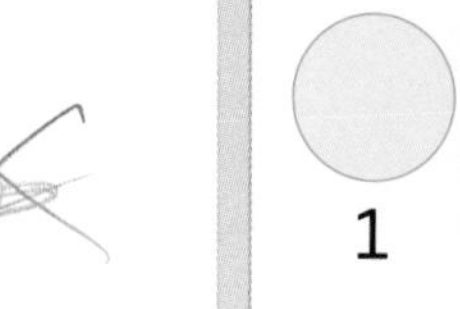

1

5. 91 − 39 = ☐

1

6. 80 ÷ 10 = ☐

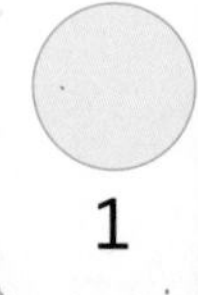

1

SET G

Test 2: Reasoning

Marks

1. Mrs Dyde's group has 5 children.

Each child has brought two items to show.

How many items does the group have to show altogether?

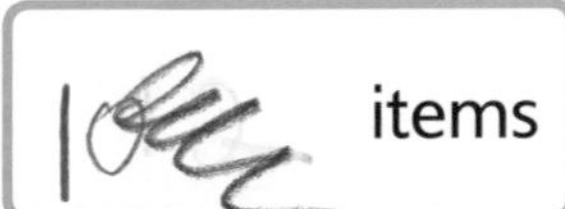

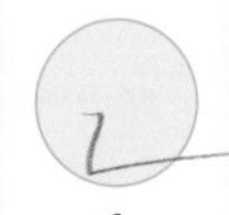

1

2. One of the shapes is in the wrong place in Josh's sorting grid.

Circle the shape that is in the wrong place.

Is a quadrilateral	Is not a quadrilateral
	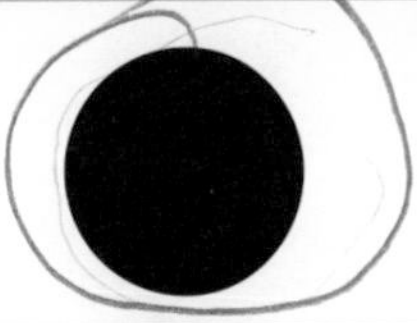

1

Marks

3. Write the correct numbers in each box.

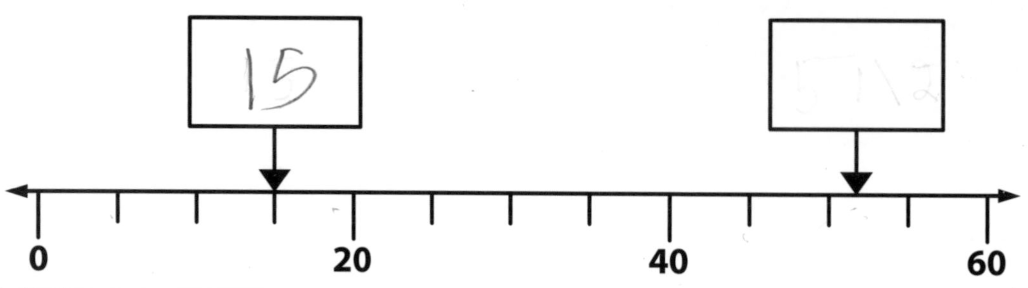

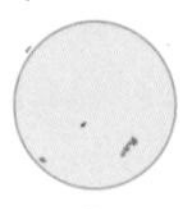
2

4. Amir is sorting number cards into odd and even groups.

Odd	Even
7 12 15 19 3	8 14 13 20 2

Two of his cards are in the wrong place. Circle them.

1

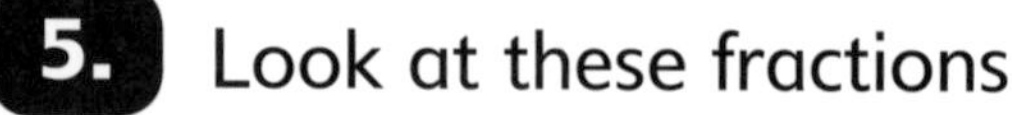

5. Look at these fractions.

$\frac{1}{2}$ $\frac{1}{4}$ $\frac{1}{3}$ $\frac{2}{4}$ $\frac{3}{4}$

Circle the two fractions that are equivalent.

1

Marks

6. Josh buys a can of fizzy drink for 60p.

Tick the coins he could use to make 60p.

Tick a different set of coins Josh could use to make 60p.

2

7. Charlotte has 60 marbles.

She gives 17 to Kian.

She gives 21 to Amir.

How many marbles does Charlotte have left?

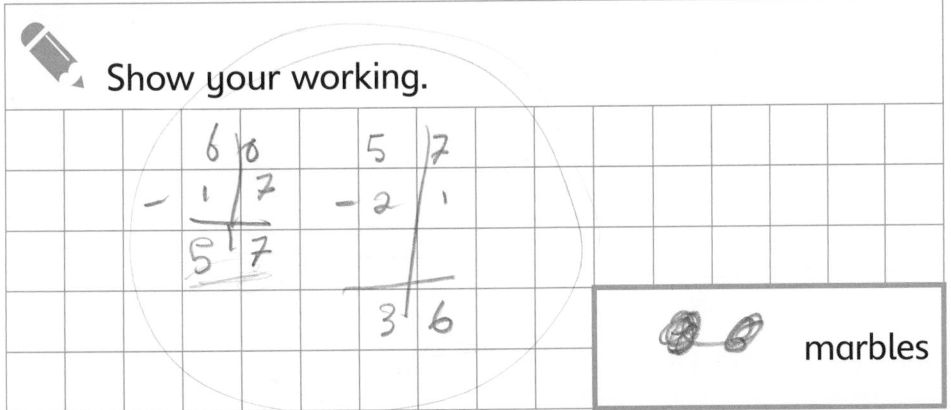

2

Well done! END OF SET G!

SET H

Test 1: Arithmetic

Marks

1. $6 + 6 =$ [12]

1

2. $9 \times 5 =$ [45]

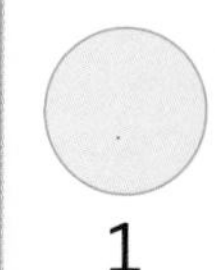

1

3. $10 + 30 + 20 =$ [60]

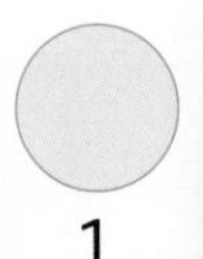

1

Marks

4. $\frac{1}{2}$ of 40 = [20]

1

5. 76 + 25 = [ ]

$$\begin{array}{r} \overset{1}{7}6 \\ +\ 25 \\ \hline 101 \end{array}$$

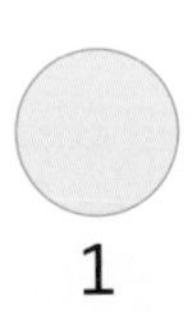

1

6. 10 ÷ 5 = [ ]

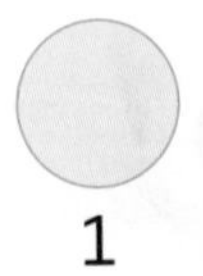

1

SET H

Test 2: Reasoning

Marks

1. How many tens are there in 89?

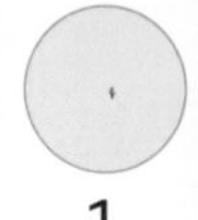

1

How many ones are there in 72?

1

2. Josh collects football stickers.

He needs 100 to complete his album.

In January, he collected 30 stickers.

In February, he collected 40 stickers.

How many stickers does he still need to collect?

1

1

Marks

3. Draw a line of symmetry on each shape.

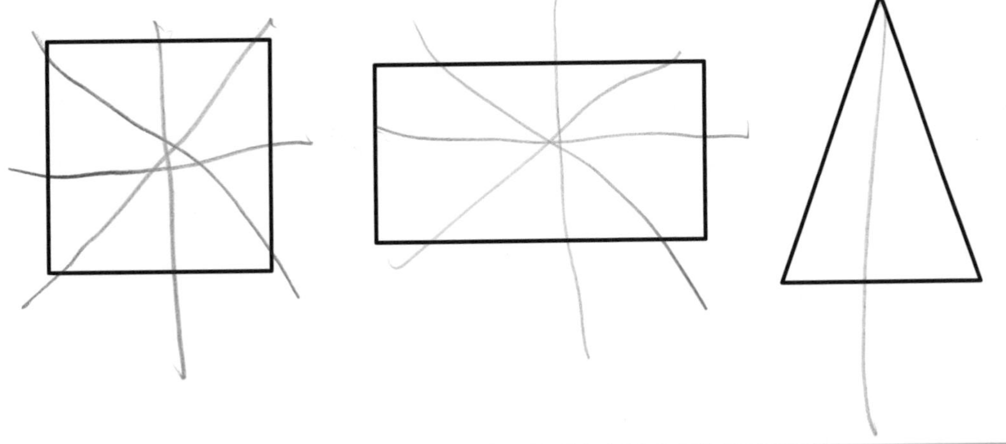

2

4. Some digits are missing from this number sentence.

Write the missing digits.

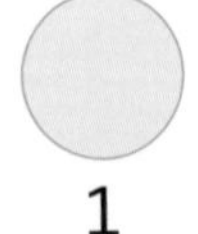

1

Marks

5. Amir is measuring out water for his class.

He has this amount of water left in his jug.

How much water is in the jug?

ml — 1

Amir pours out another 150 ml of water.

How much water is left in the jug now?

ml — 1

6. Ling planted 12 rows of potatoes.

There were 5 potatoes in each row.

A bird ate 7 of the potatoes.

How many potatoes does Ling have left?

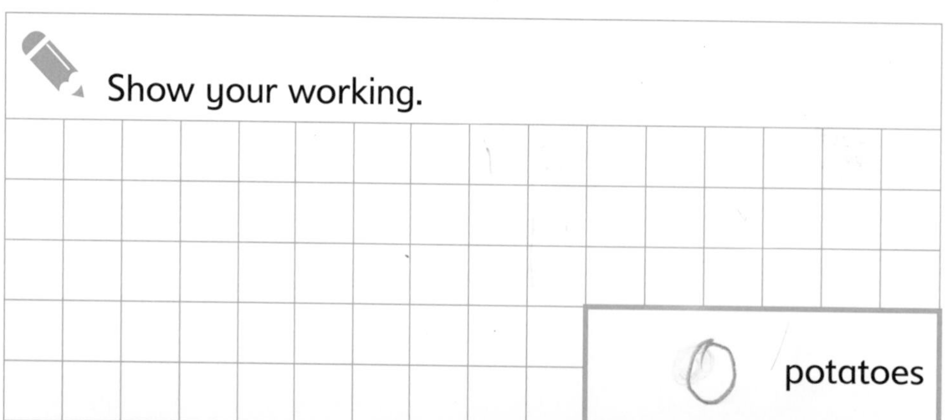

2

Well done! END OF SET H!

SET 1

Test 1: Arithmetic

Marks

1. $8 - 4 =$ ☐

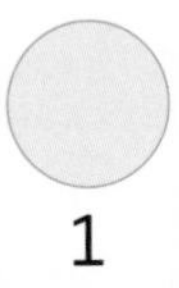
1

2. $9 \times 2 =$ ☐

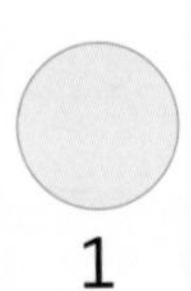
1

3. $61 -$ ☐ $= 31$

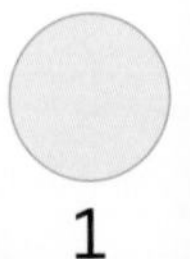
1

Marks

4. $\frac{1}{2}$ of 82 = [ ]

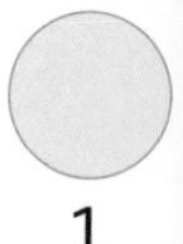

1

5. 83 − 27 = [ ]

1

6. 12 ÷ 2 = [ ]

1

SET 1

Test 2: Reasoning

Marks

1. Complete this table.

Numerals	Words
37	thirty-seven
71	Seventy - one
98	ninety-eight

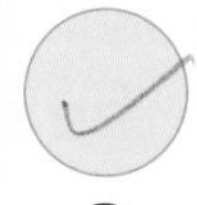

2

2. What is 10 more than 73?

1

3. One of these fractions is equivalent to $\frac{1}{2}$

Tick it.

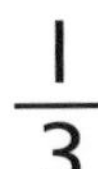

$\frac{1}{3}$ $\frac{3}{4}$ $\frac{2}{3}$ $\frac{2}{4}$

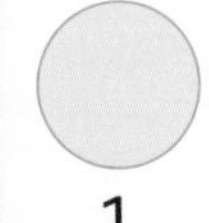

1

Marks

4. Here is Kian's toy plane.

Kian turns the plane clockwise in a three-quarter turn to the right.

Tick the plane that is in the new position.

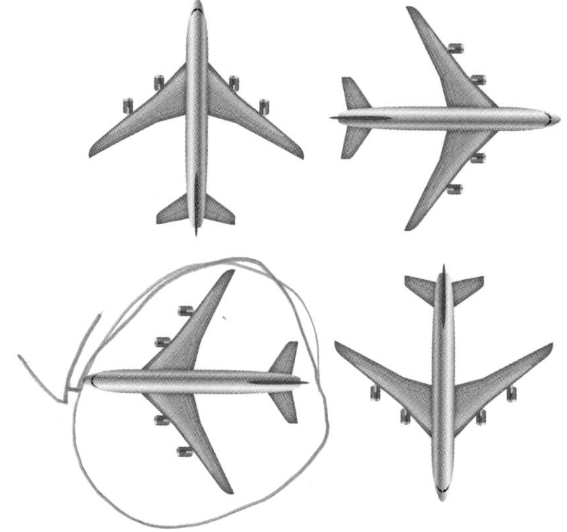

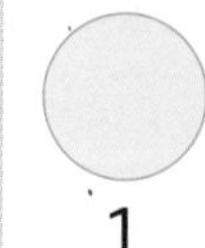

1

5. How heavy is this bag of flour?

Circle the correct measurement.

2l   1 kg   5g   1 m   100cm

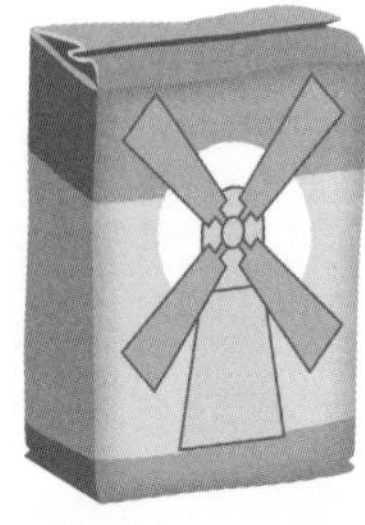

1

Marks

6. The clock shows the time that Charlotte wakes up.

What is the time? 10 ____________

1

Charlotte takes 40 minutes to get ready for school.

Draw hands on the clock to show the time when Charlotte is ready.

1

7. The table shows the different colour eyes of children in Ash Class.

Blue	6
Brown	10
Green	8
Hazel	3

How many have green or blue eyes?

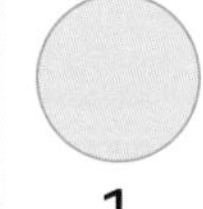
1

8. Sophie cuts a cake into 3 equal pieces.

She eats 1 piece.

What fraction of the cake does she eat?

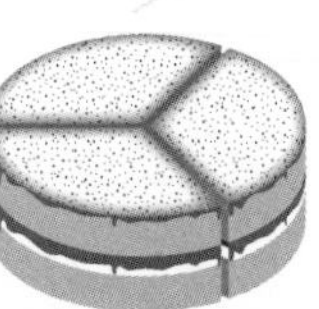

1

Well done! END OF SET 1!

Answers

Maths

Q	Mark scheme for Set A Test 1 – Arithmetic	Marks
1	5	1
2	15	1
3	4	1
4	60	1
5	70	1
6	91	1
	Total	**6**

Q	Mark scheme for Set A Test 2 – Reasoning	Marks
1	8 – 3 = 5	1
	9 + 3 = 12	1
2	17 kilograms	1
	21 kilograms	1
	Award 1 mark if child's answer = child's answer to part 1 + 4kg.	
3	These shapes ticked or clearly indicated. 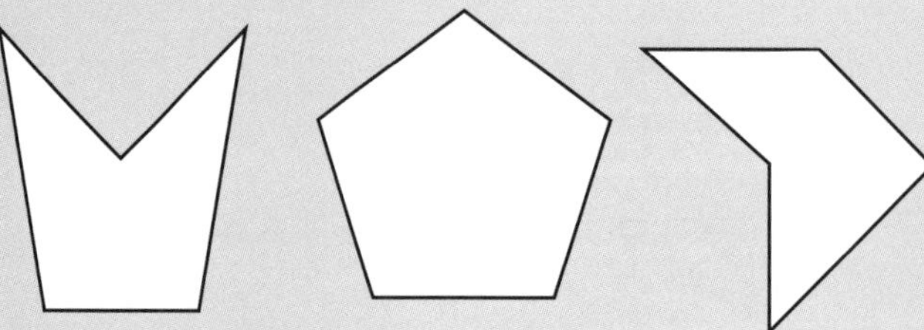 **Award 2 marks** for all three correctly identified. **Award 1 mark** for two correctly identified. Do not award the marks if other shapes are indicated, unless it is clear that the correct shapes are the child's final choice.	2

4	Lines joining fractions to number line as shown.	2

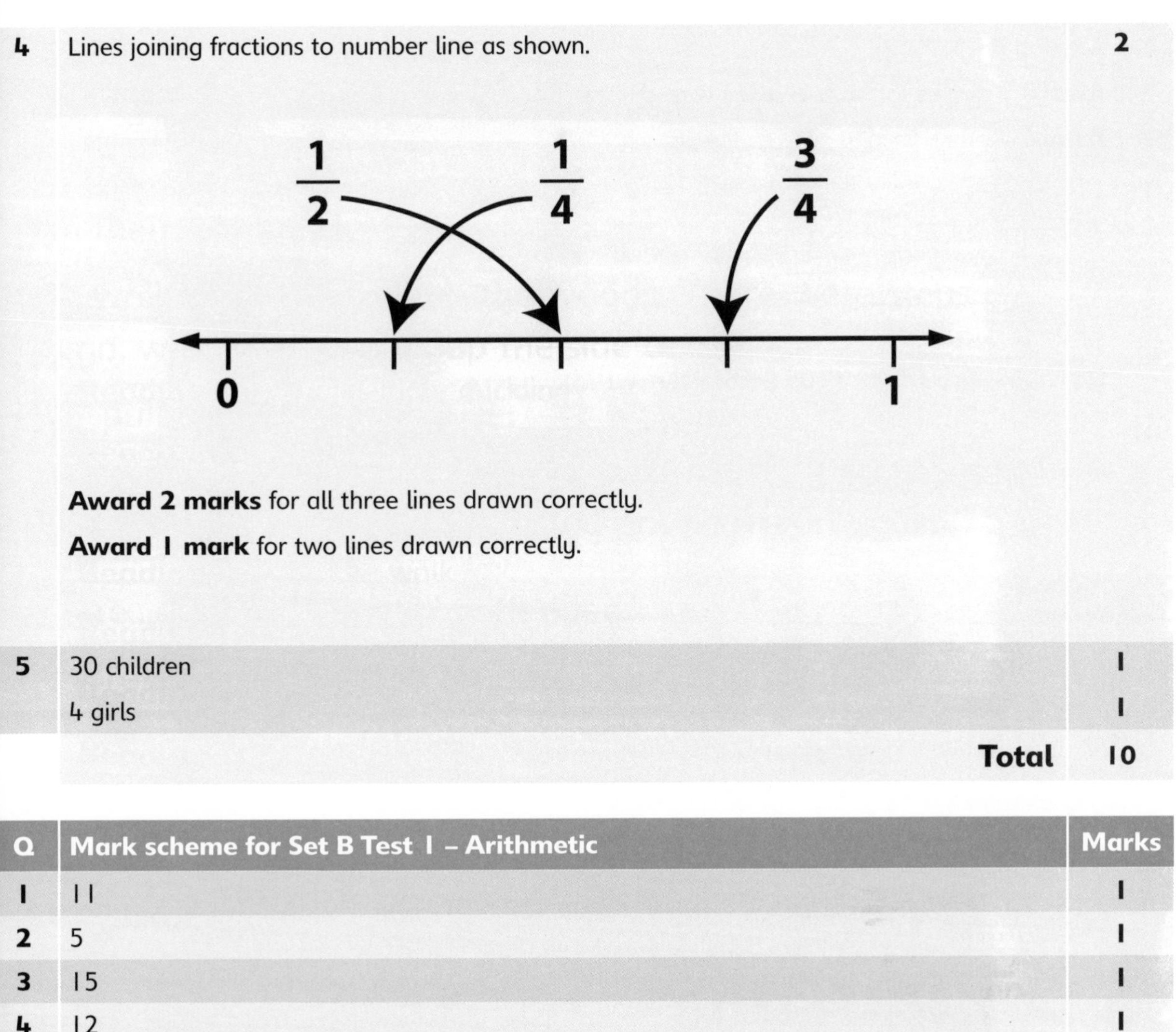

Award 2 marks for all three lines drawn correctly.

Award 1 mark for two lines drawn correctly.

5	30 children	1
	4 girls	1
	Total	**10**

Q	Mark scheme for Set B Test 1 – Arithmetic	Marks
1	11	1
2	5	1
3	15	1
4	12	1
5	9	1
6	59	1
	Total	**6**

Q	Mark scheme for Set B Test 2 – Reasoning	Marks
1		2

Shape	Number of vertices	Number of faces	Number of edges
Cylinder	0	3	2
Triangular prism	6	5	9

Award 2 marks for all four answers correct.

Award 1 mark for three answers correct.

2	3, 6, 9, 12, 15, 18, 21 **Award 2 marks** for both answers correct. **Award 1 mark** for one answer correct.	2
3	12 23 32 45 54 56	1
4	30 children	1
5	$\frac{3}{4}$	1
6	£1.05 or 105p Do not accept 1.05p or £105 (incorrect notation).	1
7	7 + 8 = 15 15 – 7 = 8	1 1
	Total	**10**

Q	Mark scheme for Set C Test 1 – Arithmetic	Marks
1	6	1
2	9	1
3	10	1
4	9	1
5	86	1
6	5	1
	Total	**6**

Q	Mark scheme for Set C Test 2 – Reasoning	Marks
1	57 34	1 1
2	15 8	1 1
3	twenty-three Accept phonetically plausible attempts. fourteen Accept phonetically plausible attempts. Spelling must be one word.	1 1
4	Kian's 6cm	1 1

5	6 cards	**1**
	18 cards	**1**
	Award 1 mark if child's answer = 24 – child's answer to part 1.	
	Total	**10**

Q	Mark scheme for Set D Test 1 – Arithmetic	Marks
1	13	**1**
2	11	**1**
3	40	**1**
4	7	**1**
5	59	**1**
6	8	**1**
	Total	**6**

Q	Mark scheme for Set D Test 2 – Reasoning	Marks
1	(see table below) **Award 2 marks** for both answers correct. **Award 1 mark** for one correct answer.	**2**
2	24	**1**
	12	**1**
3	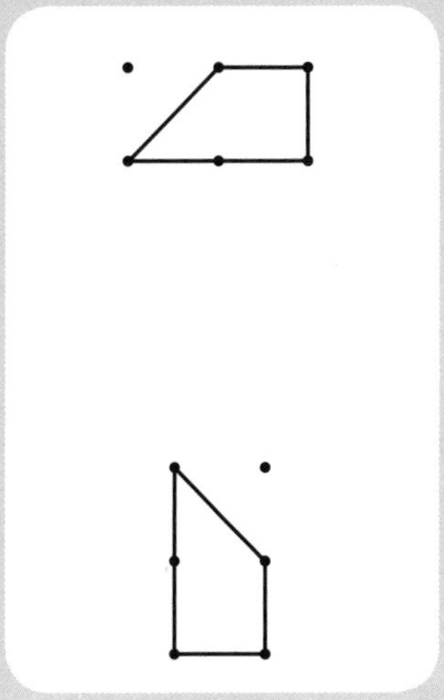	**1**
		1

10 less	Number	10 more
24	34	44
99	109	119
97	107	117

4	Hands drawn on clock face to show twenty to eleven **Award 1 mark** for the correctly positioned minute hand, which must be pointing to the 8. **Award 1 mark** for the correctly positioned hour hand, which must be between the 10 and the 11. **Award no marks**, if there is no clear difference in length between the minute and hour hands.	2
5	21 **Award 2 marks** for the correct answer. **Award 1 mark** for evidence of a correct method but with one arithmetic error, eg finding $\frac{1}{4}$ of 28 and multiplying by 3 = wrong answer.	2
	Total	**10**

Q	Mark scheme for Set E Test 1 – Arithmetic	Marks
1	5	1
2	25	1
3	100	1
4	10	1
5	60	1
6	5	1
	Total	**6**

Q	Mark scheme for Set E Test 2 – Reasoning	Marks
1	34 pens	1
2	20 pencils	1
3	12cm	1
4	Irregular pentagon ticked as shown.	1
	Rhombus ticked as shown.	1
	Accept any other clear way of indicating the correct answers. Do not award the marks if other cards are indicated unless it is clear the correct shapes are the child's final choices.	

5	4 pieces Do not accept $\frac{1}{4}$.	1
6	45p 20p	1 1
7	26 sweets **Award 2 marks** for correct answer. **Award 1 mark** evidence of a correct method but with one arithmetic error, eg 2 × 12 = wrong answer, 50 – wrong answer = .	2
	Total	10

Q	Mark scheme for Set F Test 1 – Arithmetic	Marks
1	10	1
2	6	1
3	61	1
4	1	1
5	92	1
6	4	1
	Total	6

Q	Mark scheme for Set F Test 2 – Reasoning	Marks
1	14 16 18 20 22 **Award 1 mark** for both numbers correct.	1
2	These subtractions in either order: 65 – 22 = 43 65 – 43 = 22 **Award 2 marks** for both correct. **Award 1 mark** for one correct.	2
3	5 3	1 1
4	Missing shapes drawn as shown. 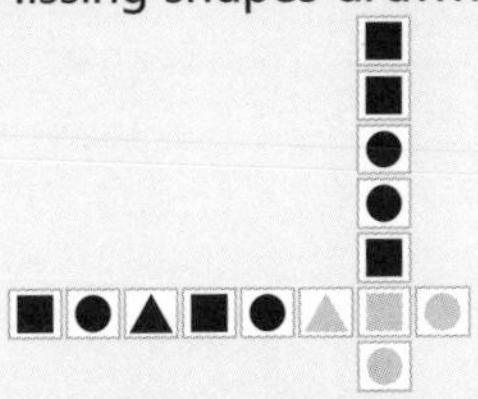 **Award 2 marks** for all four shapes correct. **Award 1 mark** for three shapes correct.	2

5	t-rex > triceratops	1
	t-rex < diplodocus	1
	21kg	1
	Total	**10**

Q	Mark scheme for Set G Test 1 – Arithmetic	Marks
1	14	1
2	4	1
3	32	1
4	18	1
5	52	1
6	8	1
	Total	**6**

Q	Mark scheme for Set G Test 2 – Reasoning	Marks
1	10 items	1
2	The irregular heptagon circled or clearly indicated. Do not award the mark if other shapes are indicated, unless it is clear that the correct shape is the child's final choice.	1
3	15 written in the first answer box as shown.	1
	52 written in the second answer box as shown.	1
	Accept any number in the range 51 to 54 inclusive.	

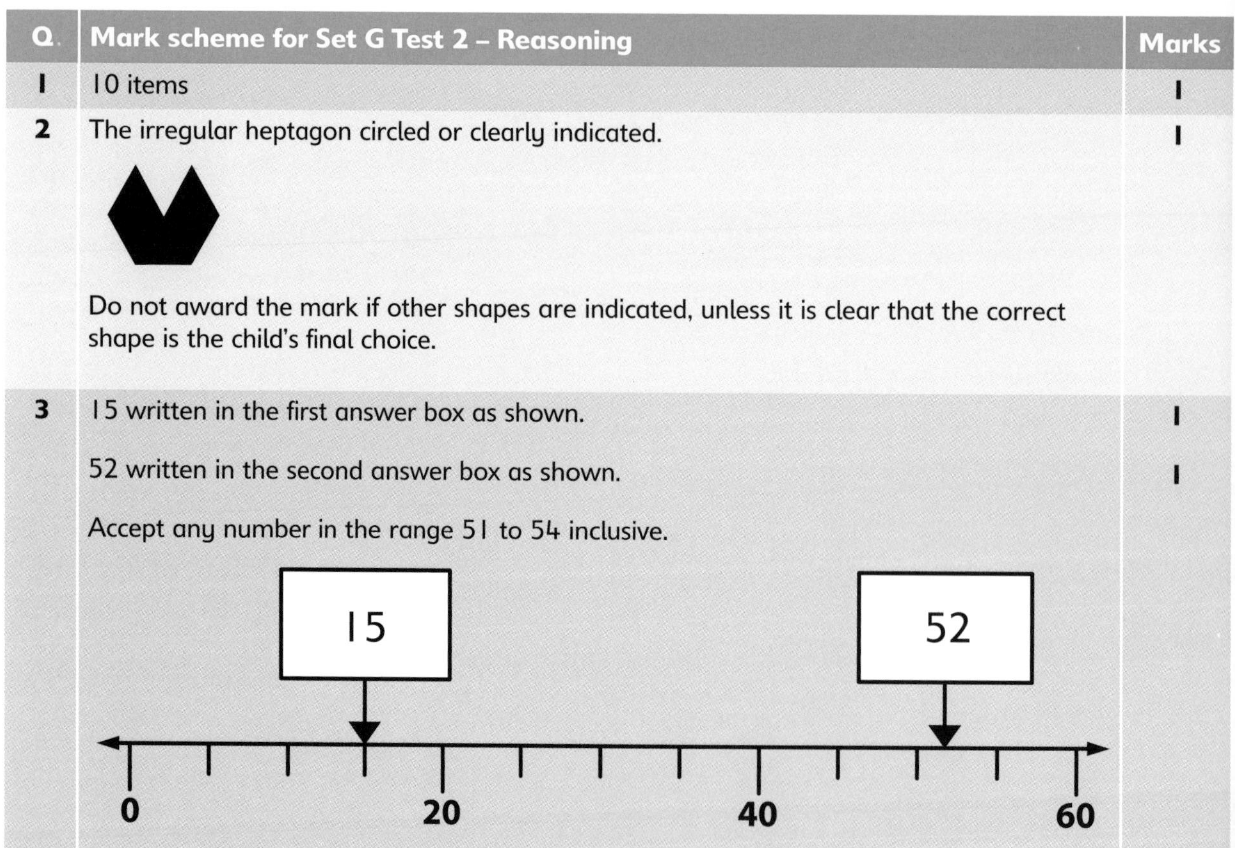

4	12 and 13 circled or clearly indicated. **Award 1 mark** only if both answers are correct. Do not award the mark if other numbers are indicated, unless it is clear that the correct numbers are the child's final choice.	1
5	$\frac{1}{2}$ and $\frac{2}{4}$ circled Do not award the mark if other fractions are indicated, unless it is clear that the correct fractions are the child's final choice.	1
6	Coins ticked to make 60p made in two different ways: 50p, 10p or 10p, 10p, 20p, 20p or 20p, 20p, 20p **Award 2 marks** for two different correct answers. **Award 1 mark** for one correct answer.	2
7	22 marbles **Award 2 marks** for correct answer. **Award 1 mark** evidence of a correct method but with one arithmetic error, eg an attempt to take away 17 and 21 from 60, but which has an arithmetic error.	2
	Total	10

Q	Mark scheme for Set H Test 1 – Arithmetic	Marks
1	12	1
2	45	1
3	60	1
4	20	1
5	101	1
6	2	1
	Total	6

Q	Mark scheme for Set H Test 2 – Reasoning	Marks
1	8 tens Do not accept 80.	1
	2 ones	1
2	30 stickers	1

3	**One** correct line of symmetry shown on each shape: 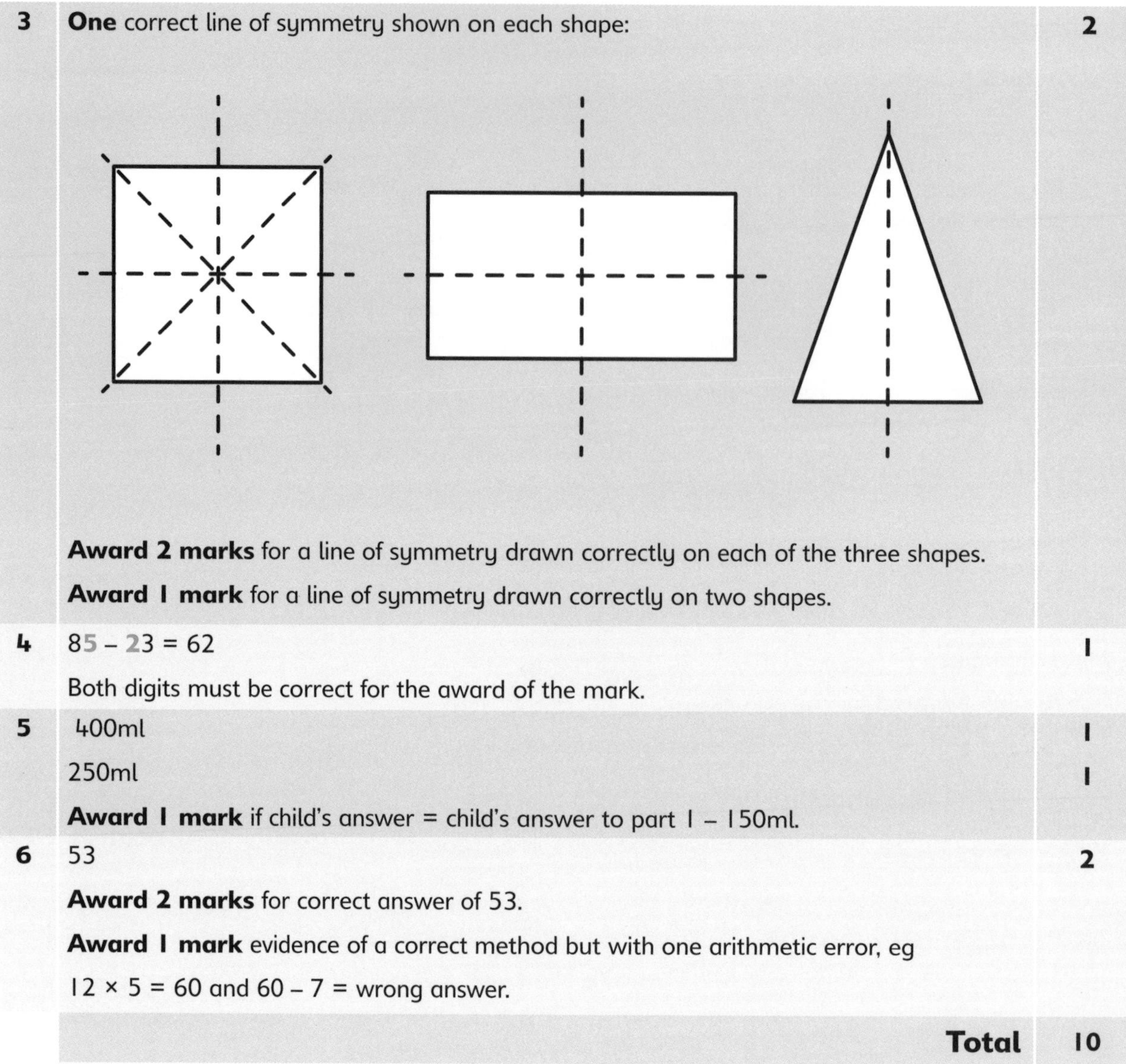 **Award 2 marks** for a line of symmetry drawn correctly on each of the three shapes. **Award 1 mark** for a line of symmetry drawn correctly on two shapes.	**2**
4	85 – 23 = 62 Both digits must be correct for the award of the mark.	**1**
5	400ml 250ml **Award 1 mark** if child's answer = child's answer to part 1 – 150ml.	**1** **1**
6	53 **Award 2 marks** for correct answer of 53. **Award 1 mark** evidence of a correct method but with one arithmetic error, eg 12 × 5 = 60 and 60 – 7 = wrong answer.	**2**
	Total	**10**

Q	Mark Scheme for Set 1 Test 1 – Arithmetic	Marks
1	4	**1**
2	18	**1**
3	30	**1**
4	41	**1**
5	56	**1**
6	6	**1**
	Total	**6**

Q	Mark Scheme for Set 1 Test 2 – Reasoning	Marks
1	<table><tr><th>Numerals</th><th>Words</th></tr><tr><td>37</td><td>thirty-seven</td></tr><tr><td>71</td><td>**seventy-one**</td></tr><tr><td>**98**</td><td>ninety-eight</td></tr></table> **Award 1 mark** for each correct answer. Accept phonetically plausible attempts.	2
2	83	1
3	$\frac{2}{4}$	1
4	This plane ticked or clearly indicated. Do not award the mark if other planes are indicated, unless it is clear that the correct plane is the child's final choice.	1
5	1 kg circled or clearly indicated. Do not award the mark if other measures are indicated, unless it is clear that the correct measure is the child's final choice.	1

6	ten past seven or seven-ten or 7.10	**1**
	Hands drawn on clock face to show ten to eight	**1**
	Award 1 mark for the correctly positioned minute hand, which must be pointing to the 10.	
	Award 1 mark for the correctly positioned hour hand, which must be between the 7 and the 8.	
	Award no marks, if there is no clear difference in length between the minute and hour hands.	
7	14 children	**1**
8	$\frac{1}{3}$	**1**
	Total	**10**

Skills check

Maths

Number and place value

I can count in steps of 2, 3, and 5 from 0 and in tens from any number forward and backward, eg what is the next number in this sequence? 78, 68, 58

I can say the place value of each digit in a two-digit number (tens and ones), eg what is the place value of the digit 8 in 78?

I can use the <, > and = signs to compare and order numbers from 0 up to 100, eg write in the correct sign to make this statement correct: 71 ☐ 87.

I can read and write numbers to at least 100 in numerals and in words, eg what is 76 written in words?

Number – addition and subtraction

I can solve problems with addition and subtraction, eg Kieron has 18 toy cars. His Mum buys him 8 more. How many cars does he have now?

I can add and subtract any two numbers that have a total of up to 20 in my head, eg 3 + 6 = 9 and I can use what I know mentally to help me find related facts to 100, eg what do you add to 30 to make 90?

I can mentally add and subtract a two-digit number and tens, eg 43 + 30 = ?

I can add and subtract a two-digit number and ones, eg 67 + 6 = ? 46 – 8 = ?

I can add and subtract two two-digit numbers, eg 56 + 37 = ?

I can add three one-digit numbers, eg 6 + 7 + 3 = ?

I can show that the addition of two numbers is commutative (that they can be done in any order) and that subtraction is not commutative,
eg I know that 34 + 25 = 59 so I also know that 25 + 34 = 59.

I can use the fact that addition and subtraction are inverses (opposite operations) and use this to help me check my calculations and solve missing number problems, eg 8 + ☐ = 12.

Skills check

Maths

Number – multiplication and division

I can recall and use multiplication and division facts for the 2, 5 and 10 multiplication tables, eg $3 \times 10 = ?$

I can recognise odd and even numbers, eg circle the odd numbers in this list: 7, 18, 29, 58, 86, 89.

I can explain that multiplication of two numbers is commutative (they can be done in any order) and division of one number by another is not commutative, eg I know that $4 \times 5 = 20$ so I also know that $5 \times 4 = 20$.

I can solve problems involving multiplication and division, eg there are 30 children in Class 2. How many tables of 5 would the teacher need so that every child has a seat and there are no spare seats?

Number – fractions

I can recognise and find the fractions $\frac{1}{3}$, $\frac{1}{4}$, $\frac{2}{4}$ and $\frac{3}{4}$ of a length or shape, eg shade in $\frac{3}{4}$ of a square.

I can recognise and find the fractions $\frac{1}{3}$, $\frac{1}{4}$, $\frac{2}{4}$ and $\frac{3}{4}$ of a set of objects or of a quantity, eg what is $\frac{3}{4}$ of 12?

I can write simple fractions, eg Mia has eaten 1 out of the 3 slices of cake. What fraction has she eaten?
I can recognise that $\frac{2}{4}$ is the same as $\frac{1}{2}$.

Measurement

I can choose and use appropriate standard units to measure:

- length/height in any direction (in m/cm)
- mass (in kg/g)
- temperature (in °C)
- capacity (in l/ml)

eg what is the length of this line?

Skills check

Maths

I can compare and order length, mass, volume/capacity using the >, < and = signs, eg make this statement correct: 86 kg □ 32 kg.

I can combine different amounts of money to make a certain value and find different combinations of coins that equal the same amounts of money, eg what coins could Mary have used to pay for an ice cream that costs £1.25?

I can tell and write the time to five minutes, including quarter past/to the hour and draw the hands on a clock face to show these times, eg draw hands on a clock face to show 2.25pm.

Geometry

I can identify and describe the properties of 2-D shapes, including the number of sides and line symmetry in a vertical line, eg how many sides does a hexagon have?

I can identify and describe the properties of 3-D shapes, including the number of edges, vertices and faces, eg how many faces does a square-based pyramid have?

I can say what 2-D shapes are on the surface of 3-D shapes, eg which 2 shapes make up the faces of a triangular prism?

I can order and arrange objects into patterns and sequences, eg what are the next 3 items in this sequence: square, circle, square, circle?

I can use mathematical vocabulary to describe position, direction and movement, and explain rotation as a turn and in terms of right angles for quarter, half and three-quarter turns, eg describe the route for the robot to exit the factory.

Statistics

I can interpret and complete simple pictograms, tally charts, block diagrams and tables, eg draw a block diagram to show the colours of eyes of children in your class.

I can ask and answer simple questions by counting the number of objects in each category and sorting the categories by quantity, eg how many children have blue eyes?

I can ask and answer questions about the total of and the difference between data, eg how many more children have blue eyes compared to brown eyes?

Progress chart

Fill in your score in the table below to see how well you've done.

	Score
SET A	14
SET B	15
SET C	5
SET D	10
SET E	11
SET F	10
SET G	10
SET H	8
SET I	10
TOTAL	93

Mark	
0–50	Good try! You need more practice in some topics – ask an adult to help you.
51–100	You're doing really well. Ask for extra help for any topics you found tricky.
101–144	You're a 10-Minute SATS maths star – good work!

You have completed all of the 10-Minute SATs Tests

Name: Snee

Date: ____________